THE POPTAIL MANUAL

OVER 90 DELICIOUS FROZEN COCKTAILS | KATHY KORDALIS

THE POPTAIL MANUAL

OVER 90 DELICIOUS FROZEN COCKTAILS | KATHY KORDALIS

hardie grant books

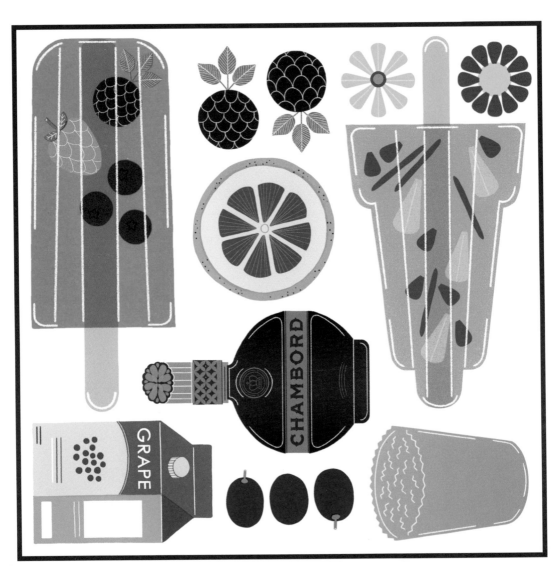

4

CONTENTS

INTRODUCTION

In essence, a poptail is a frozen cocktail. There are plenty of great ways to enjoy an alcoholic beverage: sipping out of a cup, slurping from a straw, slowly drinking a warm mug of spiked cider. But nothing beats a frozen booze stick. Whether you're looking for something creamy, fruity, spicy or fresh, you'll find there is a pop for every occasion. They are an experimental cook's dream, setting the stage for any flavour combos you can think up once you master the basics (see pages 18–23).

The Poptail Manual will guide you in your frozen cocktail journey. Here, you will find helpful tips and tricks along with some classic flavour combos to get you started. It's great to take a signature cocktail and adapt it to frozen form. Once you get the hang of it, have a play, experiment with your own combinations, and just have fun.

We hope this collection of poptail recipes inspires you to discover new and exciting ways to share and celebrate.

Part One:
THE SET-UP

THE KIT

Straightforward and easy-to-use equipment is key here. This chapter lists the essentials to get you started – you probably already have most of it at home.

⊙ THE BLENDER OR FOOD PROCESSOR

Used for blitzing, a blender or food processor will purée or emulsify fruit or veg, ensuring that all the goodness is retained. There is no need to strain – keep it all in. Texture is no bad thing, but for a smooth finish, just blitz for longer.

⊙ THE NUTRIBULLET

Also referred to as a nutrition extractor, it is often used to make whole fruit and vegetable smoothies. It can break down seeds and fruit skins, and creates velvety purées. This is an excellent tool for making whole fruit mixes for poptails.

⌃ THE GLASS JUG

A glass jug is preferred but not mandatory. Glass is best because it doesn't absorb flavours or smells. A jug with measurements is extra useful.

⌃ CHOPPING BOARD

It's best to use a chopping board solely for fruit and veg. We don't want our poptails tasting like garlic!

⊙ CITRUS SQUEEZER OR PRESS

Works best to extract every last drop of citrus juice. Waste not, want not.

⊙ DIGITAL SCALES

The most accurate way to weigh ingredients, including liquids. 1 ml is equivalent to 1 g.

⊙ MICROPLANE OR FINE GRATER

The peel of citrus fruit contains loads of flavour; it's all in the citrus oil. Finely grating the zest into poptail mixtures further enhances the taste. A Microplane grater, fine grater or box grater all work well.

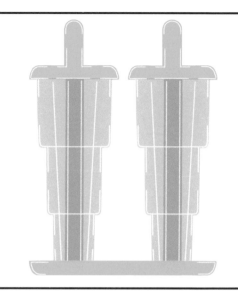

⊙ POPTAIL MOULDS

Most ice-lolly moulds make 6–10 pops and include a stick holder, so these are the easiest moulds to use. As a standard, each poptail mould holds 70 ml (2¼ fl oz); however, they come in a range of sizes and quantities. In this book, each recipe makes around 500–700 ml (17–23½ fl oz) of mixture. As well as the plastic ice-lolly moulds, you can use small and large silicone ice-cube trays, silicon cupcake cases, canapé cups, yoghurt pots, and other suitable waterproof containers.

FREEZE
FUNDAMENTALS

Learning the fundamentals of freezing will ensure that you can create any poptail you can imagine without mishaps or mess.

1

As poptails contain alcohol, their melting point is lower than that of water, so they are best kept in the freezer until the very last minute before eating. Remember that poptails will have a softer texture than booze-free ice lollies.

2

When pouring the mixture into your moulds, try to leave 5 mm (¼ in) from the top of the mould for the mixture to expand when frozen.

3

To make layered poptails, you will need some extra time. For a clean line, each layer will need to set completely before adding the next. If you want softer lines, add the second layer when the first is only partially frozen. Keep the ingredients chilled in between layers for a quicker freezing time.

4

To eliminate air bubbles in creamy poptails, partially fill the mould, give it a few taps on the counter and then continue to fill.

5

If your poptail mould has built-in stick holders, you can slide the sticks in as soon as the mixture is poured, then freeze. If your moulds don't have stick holders, simply freeze the pops for about 30–60 minutes, then insert the sticks. This will help the stick stand up straight. The best way to release the popsicles from the moulds is to flip them over and run them under warm water (not hot!).

6

The time it takes to freeze pops varies and depends on both the recipe and your freezer. Read the recipe before starting and prepare your poptails at least 12–24 hours before serving.

ALCOHOL IN POPS

When composing a poptail, avoid using more than 20 per cent alcohol or a ratio of four parts water to one part alcohol for the recipe – any more and the pops won't freeze and will fall apart when unmoulding.

Alcohol does actually freeze, just not at the temperatures that home freezers are kept at.

Ethanol, the alcohol found in beer, wine, and liqueurs, has a melting point of −114°C (−173°F). That melting point represents the temperature at which ethanol passes from a frozen solid to a liquid state.

Most home freezers maintain temperatures between −23°C (−9°F) and −18°C (0°F) in order to properly store food. Since this is much warmer than −114°C (−173°F), ethanol will remain liquid. However, the rest of the poptail ingredients will still freeze, so you can enjoy a solid frozen treat!

POP FLAVOUR PROFILES

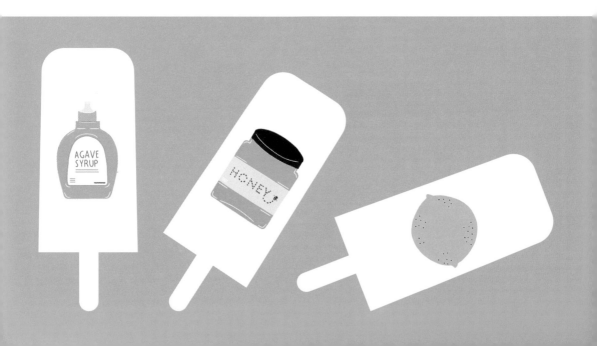

To create a sophisticated, well-rounded flavour profile, ensure that your pop has a good balance of sweet, bitter and sour flavours.

SWEET

Traditionally, cocktails are sweetened with simple syrup (see page 31), which helps to take the edge off the sour and bitter notes. This addition can transform a poptail. As sweetness is dulled when frozen, it's best to add more syrup than you would to an unfrozen cocktail.

If you prefer, you can also use

a sweetener that naturally comes as a liquid, such as one of the following options.

AGAVE SYRUP

Made from the agave plant (which also gives us tequila), this syrup has slightly more calories than white sugar but is about 25 per cent sweeter, so you can get away with less of it. Plus, agave nectar does good things for your gut. It contains a type of dietary fibre, known as a prebiotic, that nourishes intestinal bacteria. Dark agave nectar has stronger caramel notes, and imparts a delicious, distinct flavour to many desserts. Light agave nectar has a mild, neutral flavour.

HONEY

This kitchen staple provides a concentrated dose of antioxidants, and is said to promote heart health. Honey is also naturally antibacterial, because the bees add an enzyme that makes hydrogen peroxide.

STEVIA

The powdered extract of the South American stevia plant is a zero-calorie sugar substitute that's 100 per cent natural. While it's 200–300 times sweeter than sugar, stevia doesn't cause a spike in blood glucose levels – sparing you the crash that follows a spoonful of the white stuff. Make sure you follow the packet instructions to substitute sugar or syrup with the right amount of stevia.

COCONUT BLOSSOM SYRUP

Produced from the sap of the coconut palm's flower buds, coconut palm sugar has a glycaemic index rating of 35, much lower than refined sugar. It contains amino acids, potassium, magnesium, zinc, iron and B vitamins.

XYLITOL

'Xyl' is the Greek for 'wood', and xylitol was first made from Finnish birch trees in the early 1900s. It is naturally produced by most living things including trees, fruits and plants, and has recently taken off as a sweetener – perhaps because it has 40 per cent fewer calories than sugar, 75 per cent less carbohydrates and a low GI of 7. It also is thought to inhibit the bacteria in the mouth that causes tooth decay. What's more, xylitol does not cause a spike in blood sugar or insulin levels and is believed to be helpful in reducing sugar cravings.

COCONUT BLOSSOM SYRUP

BITTER

Bitters, such as Angostura bitters, are a type of spirit or mixer used to make cocktails dry and add a bitter, or bittersweet, touch. Bitters are botanically infused and were originally developed to relieve stomach problems, nausea and other physical problems.

Today, there is a resurgence in the use of bitters in cocktails, and poptails are a perfect vehicle for this flavour profile. If you had to choose one bitters as a mixer, the one to use is Angostura Aromatic Bitters. It was first made in 1824 in the town of Angostura, Venezuela made with over 40 ingredients including water, vegetable flavouring extracts, and a bitter root called gentian.

It also imparts a great flavour to soups, salads, vegetables, gravies, fish, meat, fruit juices, grapefruit, fruit salad, stewed prunes and figs, preserved fruits, jellies and sherbets.

SOUR

The addition of a sour note cuts through any cloying sweetness and introduces an interesting dimension to the final taste. Here, keeping it simple is the best policy. Citrus is the best way to go. Lemons, limes or grapefruit work best in pops. Taste, taste and taste again to achieve the flavour profile that best suits you.

SYRUP

If you decide to use a sugar-based syrup to flavour your poptails, the standard recipe overleaf can be made and then kept in your fridge for up to 4 weeks. It has many other uses too: brush onto cakes to keep them moist or add to crushed berries to make a fruit coulis. You can infuse the syrup with any flavour you like; try adding vanilla seeds or essence, lemongrass, ginger or any kind of herb. The possibilities are endless.

SIMPLE SYRUP

Makes 250 ml (8½ fl oz)

Ingredients
250 ml (8½ fl oz) boiling water
100 g (3½ oz) golden caster (superfine)
  sugar

Method
Stir the boiling water and sugar
together until the sugar has completely
dissolved. Add your choice of
flavourings and leave to cool. To store
the syrup, pour into sterilised jars,
screw on the lids and chill. It will keep
for up to 4 weeks in the fridge.

GINGER SYRUP

Makes 250 ml (8½ fl oz)

Ingredients
250 ml (8½ fl oz) boiling water
100 g (3½ oz) golden caster (superfine)
  sugar
large piece (about 30 g/1 oz) fresh
  ginger, peeled and cut into very thin
  rounds

Method
Stir the boiling water and sugar
together until the sugar has completely
dissolved. Add the ginger and leave
until cool. To store the syrup, pour into
sterilised jars, screw on the lids and
chill. It will keep for up to 4 weeks in
the fridge.

Part Two: THE POPTAIL LIST

FRESH
AND FRUITY

Fresh, fruity, tangy, colourful, vibrant...
summer in the garden. These poptails are
relatively easy and quick – no fancy infusions
or too many types of liqueur. Just simple.

LIMONCELLO BASIL POPS

SERVES 8
These bold, zingy popsicles made with Italian Limoncello and basil are a fun ending for your summer parties.

❶ INGREDIENTS

420 ML (14 FL OZ) BOILING WATER
4 TBSP XYLITOL • ZEST AND JUICE OF 3 LEMONS
120 ML (4 FL OZ) LIMONCELLO • PINCH OF SALT
16 BASIL LEAVES

❷ EQUIPMENT

MEASURING JUG   ZESTER   8 POPSICLE MOULDS & STICKS

❸ METHOD

Pour the boiling water from the kettle into a jug and mix in the xylitol to dissolve. Let it cool, then stir through the lemon zest and juice, Limoncello and salt. Divide the mixture between the moulds, then slide 2 basil leaves into each one. Place the lid on the tray, and insert the sticks. Freeze for 12–14 hours, until solid.

MELON, LIME & MINT TEQUILA POPS

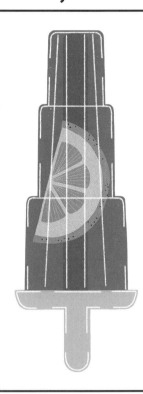

❶ INGREDIENTS

1 GALIA MELON, PEELED AND DESEEDED
(APPROX. 330 G/11½ OZ CLEANED WEIGHT)
2 LIMES (1 JUICED AND 1 SLICED INTO 16 HALF MOONS)
150 ML (5 FL OZ) TEQUILA • 1 LARGE HANDFUL MINT
100 ML (3½ FL OZ) LIGHT AGAVE SYRUP

❷ EQUIPMENT

BLENDER   DIGITAL   MEASURING   8 POPSICLE
           SCALES   JUG   MOULDS & STICKS

❸ METHOD

Blitz the melon and lime juice in a blender to form a purée. Strain into a jug through a fine mesh sieve to remove any seeds and bits. Stir in the tequila, mint and agave syrup. Divide the mixture between the popsicle moulds and freeze for 30 minutes. Place the lid on the tray, and insert the sticks. Freeze for a further 12–14 hours, until solid.

SERVES 8

Blending fresh melon, a squeeze of lime and a kick of tequila, these promise to be a truly refreshing treat.

APPLE POP

❶ INGREDIENTS

500 ML (17 FL OZ) CLOUDY APPLE JUICE
30 G (1 OZ) COCONUT BLOSSOM SYRUP
100 ML (3½ FL OZ) APPLE LIQUEUR
1 GREEN APPLE, VERY THINLY SLICED

❷ EQUIPMENT

DIGITAL SCALES   MEASURING JUG   KNIFE   8 POPSICLE MOULDS & STICKS

❸ METHOD

In a jug, mix the apple juice, coconut blossom syrup and apple liqueur. Pour into the moulds and freeze for 1 hour. Then slide the apple slices into each mould and freeze for a further 12–14 hours, until solid.

SERVES 8
Sweet, sour and fresh apple flavours are combined in this delicious pop.

WATERMELON MOJITO

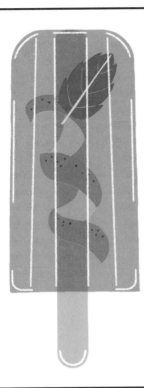

SERVES 8
Nothing says summertime quite like watermelon and mojitos, so this one is a no-brainer.

❶ INGREDIENTS

500 G (1 LB 2 OZ) SEEDLESS WATERMELON, CUT INTO CHUNKS
1 BUNCH MINT, TOUGH STEMS REMOVED, RESERVING 8 LEAVES TO SERVE
50 ML (1¾ FL OZ) COCONUT BLOSSOM SYRUP
1 LIME, PLUS 8 PEEL STRIPS
100 ML (3½ FL OZ) WHITE RUM

❷ EQUIPMENT

| DIGITAL SCALES | BLENDER | MEASURING JUG | 8 POPSICLE MOULDS & STICKS |

❸ METHOD

In a blender or food processor, blitz the watermelon, mint, coconut blossom syrup and the flesh of the lime until smooth. Pour into a jug and mix in the rum. Divide the mixture between the popsicle moulds, place the lid on the tray and freeze for 30 minutes. Then add the lime peel and reserved mint leaves to each pop, followed by the sticks, and freeze for a further 12–14 hours, until solid.

BERRY GRAPEFRUIT ROSÉ SANGRIA

A blushing rosé sangria – light, lively and pink! The grapefruit adds tartness and bitterness to create a perfect balance.

SERVES 8

❶ INGREDIENTS ....

60 g (2 oz) honey

200 ml (7 fl oz) rosé

200 ml (7 fl oz) grapefruit juice

150 ml (5 fl oz) club soda

150 g (5 oz) mixed berries

❷ EQUIPMENT
measuring jug
digital scales
8 popsicle moulds
8 popsicle sticks

❸ METHOD
In a jug, mix the honey, rosé, grapefruit juice and club soda. Drop a mixture of berries into each mould and divide the sangria mixture between the popsicle moulds. Place the lid on the tray and freeze for 30 minutes. Then slide the popsicle sticks into the lid slots and freeze for a further 12–14 hours, until solid.

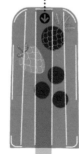

ZULU WARRIOR POP

This Zulu warrior pop is made with Midori liqueur and strawberries – you'll be ready to go into battle. This recipe needs to be made a day in advance.

SERVES 8

❶ INGREDIENTS ....

60 ml (2 fl oz) Midori

300 g (10½ oz) green melon

60 ml (2 fl oz) vodka

300 ml (10 fl oz) orange juice

8 strawberries, sliced

❷ EQUIPMENT
blender
measuring jug
digital scales
8 popsicle moulds
8 popsicle sticks

❸ METHOD
In a blender or food processor, blitz the Midori and green melon until smooth and store in the fridge. In a jug, mix the vodka and orange juice, then divide the mixture between the popsicle moulds. Place the lid on the tray and freeze for 30 minutes. Add the sliced strawberries to the moulds and freeze for 12–14 hours, until solid. Top with the melon mixture. Then slide the popsicle sticks into the lid slots and freeze for a further 12–14 hours, until solid.

LYCHEE TROP POP

It's time to bust out the tropical flavours of lychee, pineapple and passion fruit – spiked with vodka.

SERVES 8

❶ INGREDIENTS

100 ml (3½ fl oz) vodka

1 × 425 g tin lychees, drained

300 ml (10 fl oz) pineapple juice

4 passion fruits, pulp reserved

❷ EQUIPMENT
blender
measuring jug
digital scales
8 popsicle moulds
8 popsicle sticks

❸ METHOD
In a blender or food processor, blitz the vodka, lychees and pineapple juice until smooth. Pour into a jug, then add the passion fruit. Divide the mixture between the popsicle moulds, place the lid on the tray, and freeze for 30 minutes. Then slide the popsicle sticks into the lid slots and freeze for a further 12–14 hours, until solid.

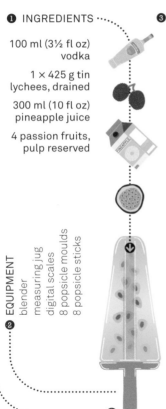

RED VELVET

A spiked dessert on a stick! No artificial red colouring here – only natural ingredients so it's good for you, too.

SERVES 8

❶ INGREDIENTS

50 ml (1¾ fl oz) light agave syrup

300 g (10½ oz) mixed red berries (fresh or frozen)

200 ml (7 fl oz) Champagne

2 teaspoons vanilla paste

10 ml (¼ fl oz) Chambord

❷ EQUIPMENT
blender
measuring jug
digital scales
8 popsicle moulds
8 popsicle sticks

❸ METHOD
In a blender or food processor, blitz the syrup and berries into a purée and pour the mixture into a jug. Add the Champagne, vanilla paste and Chambord to the jug and mix well. Divide the mixture between the popsicle moulds, place the lid on the tray, and freeze for 30 minutes. Then slide the popsicle sticks into the lid slots and freeze for a further 12–14 hours, until solid.

PIMM'S POP

English summer in a frozen cocktail with strawberries, cucumber and fresh mint.

SERVES 8

Ingredients
100 ml (3½ fl oz) Pimm's
500 ml (17 fl oz) sugar-free lemonade
1 cucumber, sliced into rounds
8 strawberries, hulled and thinly sliced
1 handful mint leaves

Equipment
measuring jug, digital scales, 8 popsicle moulds, 8 wooden popsicle sticks

Method
In a jug, mix the Pimm's and lemonade and set aside. Place the cucumber, strawberry slices and mint into the moulds. Divide the mixture between the popsicle moulds, place the lid on the tray and slide the popsicle sticks into the lid slots. Freeze for 12–14 hours, until solid.

PINEAPPLE HIBISCUS

Citrusy, sour hibiscus balances the pineapple.

SERVES 8

Ingredients
1 small pineapple, peeled and roughly chopped
100 ml (3½ fl oz) Bacardi
200 ml (7 fl oz) brewed hibiscus tea
juice of 1 lime
2 tablespoons hibiscus syrup, plus
  8 hibiscus flowers

Equipment
blender or food processor, measuring jug, digital scales, 8 popsicle moulds, 8 wooden popsicle sticks

Method
Set aside 8 chunks of pineapple and blitz the remaining pineapple with the Bacardi, hibiscus tea, lime juice and hibiscus syrup until smooth. Place the reserved pinapple and the hibiscus flowers in the moulds and insert the sticks. Divide the mixture between the moulds and freeze for 12–14 hours, until solid.

BLOOD ORANGE APEROL

Blood orange, with its deep red flesh, imparts a more intense flavour than the traditional orange and marries well with the Aperol.

SERVES 8

Ingredients
500 ml (17 fl oz) blood orange juice
100 ml (3½ fl oz) Aperol
100 g (3½ oz) runny honey
1 blood orange, thinly sliced

Equipment
measuring jug, digital scales, 8 popsicle moulds, 8 wooden popsicle sticks

Method
In a jug, mix the blood orange juice, Aperol and runny honey until well combined. Divide the mixture between the popsicle moulds, place the lid on the tray, and freeze for 30 minutes. Then add the orange slices to each pop, slide the popsicle sticks into the lid slots and freeze for a further 12–14 hours, until solid.

GUAVA, GIN & DRAGON FRUIT

This is just plain pretty, light and delicate. Simplicity itself!

SERVES 8

Ingredients
500 ml (17 fl oz) guava juice
60 ml (2 fl oz) coconut blossom syrup
100 ml (3½ fl oz) gin
1 dragon fruit, peeled and thinly sliced

Equipment
measuring jug, digital scales, 8 popsicle moulds, 8 wooden popsicle sticks

Method
In a jug, mix the guava juice, coconut blossom syrup and gin. Divide the mixture between the popsicle moulds, place the lid on the tray, and freeze for 30 minutes. Then add the dragon fruit slices, slide the popsicle sticks into the lid slots and freeze for a further 12–14 hours, until solid.

REFRESHINGLY
COOL

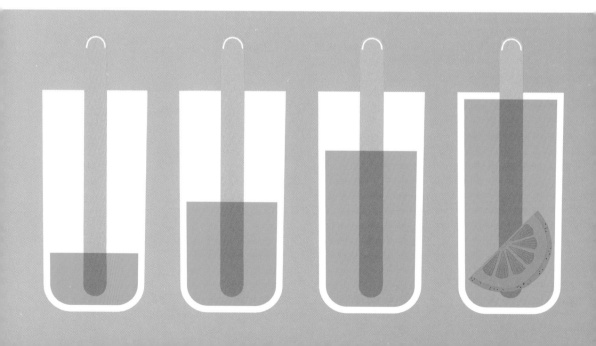

These are guaranteed to impress any discerning guest. Simple, stylish and just plain cool.

GREEN TEA & WHISKEY

❶ INGREDIENTS

4 GREEN TEABAGS
500 ML (17 FL OZ) HOT WATER
100 ML (3½ FL OZ) AGAVE SYRUP
100 ML (3½ FL OZ) WHISKEY

❷ EQUIPMENT

DIGITAL SCALES | MEASURING JUG | 6 SILICON MUFFIN CASES | 6 WOODEN SPOONS

❸ METHOD

In a heatproof glass jug, infuse the green tea in the hot water. Add the agave syrup and leave for 1–2 hours. Discard the tea bags, stir in the whiskey and pour into the muffin cases. Place on a tray in the freezer for 1 hour. Remove from the freezer and put a wooden spoon in each case, then freeze for a further 12–14 hours, until solid.

SERVES 6

Green tea and whiskey is as popular in China as gin and tonic is in England. It is loaded with antioxidants and nutrients that have powerful effects on the body.

ENGLISH GARDEN POPS

SERVES 8
With a hint of elderflower and cool cucumber, this pop is made for long, hot summer nights spent in a garden.

❶ INGREDIENTS

120 ML (4 FL OZ) GIN
500 ML (17 FL OZ) APPLE AND ELDERFLOWER JUICE
JUICE OF 1 LIME
1 SMALL CUCUMBER, THINLY SLICED LENGTHWAYS
8 MINT LEAVES

❷ EQUIPMENT

DIGITAL SCALES   MEASURING JUG   8 POPSICLE MOULDS & STICKS

❸ METHOD

In a jug, mix the gin, apple and elderflower juice and lime juice. Place 1–2 strips of cucumber in each popsicle mould and add a mint leaf to each. Divide the mixture between the moulds, place the lid on the tray and freeze for 30 minutes before sliding in the popsicle sticks. Freeze for a further 12–14 hours, until solid.

GRAPEFRUIT & CUCUMBER POP

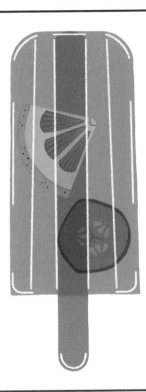

❶ INGREDIENTS

100 ML (3½ FL OZ) GIN
400 ML (13½ FL OZ) GRAPEFRUIT JUICE,
PLUS ⅓ GRAPEFRUIT, SLICED
100 ML (3½ FL OZ) LIGHT AGAVE SYRUP
3 CUCUMBERS, 2 ROUGHLY CHOPPED
AND 1 THINLY SLICED
1 LIME, PEELED
150 ML (5 FL OZ) CLUB SODA

❷ EQUIPMENT

DIGITAL   BLENDER   8 POPSICLE
SCALES   MOULDS & STICKS

❸ METHOD

In a blender, blitz the gin, grapefruit juice,
agave syrup, cucumber and lime flesh until
smooth. Add the club soda and mix well.
Divide the mixture between the moulds, place
the lid on the tray, and freeze for 30 minutes.
Then add the grapefruit and cucumber slices,
slide in the popsicle sticks and freeze for a
further 12–14 hours.

SERVES 8
Both grapefruit and cucumber are extremely
hydrating, so this pop is a super
refreshing treat.

KING'S JUBILEE

❶ INGREDIENTS

100 ML (3½ FL OZ) LEMON JUICE
100 ML (3½ FL OZ) BACARDI
50 ML (1¾ FL OZ) MARASCHINO CHERRY SYRUP
50 ML (1¾ FL OZ) LIGHT AGAVE SYRUP
200 ML (7 FL OZ) CLUB SODA
12 MARASCHINO CHERRIES

❷ EQUIPMENT

DIGITAL SCALES   MEASURING JUG   12 MINI POPSICLE MOULDS & STICKS

❸ METHOD

In a jug, mix the lemon juice, Bacardi, Maraschino and agave syrups. Top with the club soda. Divide the mixture between the popsicle moulds, place the lid on the tray, and freeze for 30 minutes. Then add the Maraschino cherries to each pop, slide the popsicle sticks into the lid slots and freeze for a further 12–14 hours, until solid.

MAKES 12 MINIPOPS
This classic was adapted from the Café Royal Cocktail Book, published in 1937. It has lemon zing and a Maraschino cherry.

PURPLE GRAPE

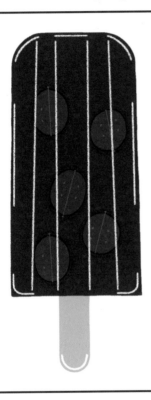

SERVES 8
A powerful purple pop that
packs a punch.

❶ INGREDIENTS

500 ML (17 FL OZ) PURPLE GRAPE JUICE
50 G (1¾ OZ) RUNNY HONEY
JUICE OF 1 LEMON
100 ML (3½ FL OZ) VODKA
16 SEEDLESS PURPLE GRAPES, HALVED

❷ EQUIPMENT

DIGITAL   MEASURING   8 POPSICLE
SCALES   JUG   MOULDS & STICKS

❸ METHOD

In a jug, mix the grape juice, runny honey,
lemon juice and vodka. Divide the mixture
between popsicle moulds, place the lid on the
tray, and freeze for 30 minutes. Then drop a
few sliced grapes into each mould, slide the
popsicle sticks into the lid slots and freeze for
a further 12–14 hours, until solid.

TRANSFUSION

❶ INGREDIENTS

100 ML (3½ FL OZ) VODKA
60 ML (2 FL OZ) GINGER SYRUP (SEE RECIPE ON PAGE 31)
JUICE OF 1 LIME
300 ML (10 FL OZ) PURPLE GRAPE JUICE
250 ML (8½ FL OZ) CLUB SODA

❷ EQUIPMENT

DIGITAL SCALES MEASURING JUG 12 MINI POPSICLE MOULDS & STICKS

❸ METHOD

In a jug, mix the vodka, ginger syrup, lime juice, grape juice and club soda. Divide the mixture between popsicle moulds, place the lid on the tray, and freeze for 30 minutes. Then slide the popsicle sticks into the lid slots and freeze for a further 12–14 hours, until solid.

MAKES 12 MINIPOPS
The Transfusion is a club standard made with vodka, ginger ale and grape juice. This twist on the classic replaces the ale with a ginger syrup.

OLIVE MARTINI

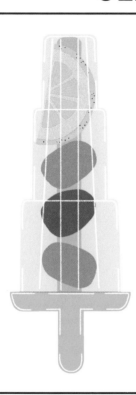

30 ML (1 FL OZ) GIN • 70 ML (2¼ FL OZ) VERMOUTH
100 G (3½ OZ) RUNNY HONEY
500 ML (17 FL OZ) CLUB SODA
8–24 PITTED GREEN OLIVES
8 LEMON SLICES

② EQUIPMENT

DIGITAL   MEASURING   8 POPSICLE
SCALES   JUG   MOULDS & STICKS

③ METHOD

In a jug, mix the gin, vermouth, honey and club soda. Thread each popsicle stick with 1-3 olives (depending on taste), followed by a lemon slice. Divide the gin mixture between the popsicle moulds, place the lid on the tray, and freeze for 30 minutes. Then slide the olive sticks into the slots and freeze for a further 12–14 hours, until solid.

SERVES 8
Based on a Dirty Martini, which uses olive brine or olive juice for an additional kick.

KAMIKAZE

❶ INGREDIENTS

80 ML (2½ FL OZ) VODKA
20 ML (¾ FL OZ) TRIPLE SEC
2 LEMONS (JUICE OF 1 AND 1 THINLY SLICED)
400 ML (13½ FL OZ) CLOUDY LEMONADE

❷ EQUIPMENT

DIGITAL SCALES

MEASURING JUG

8 POPSICLE MOULDS & STICKS

❸ METHOD

In a jug, mix the vodka, triple sec, lemon juice and cloudy lemonade. Divide the mixture between the popsicle moulds, place the lid on the tray, and freeze for 30 minutes. Then add the lemon slices to the moulds before sliding the popsicle sticks into the lid slots. Freeze for a further 12–14 hours, until solid.

MAKES 12 MINIPOPS
This vibrant pop will remind you of school days with its fresh lemonade taste.

APEROL SPRITZ SHAVED ICE

SERVES 8
A light, fresh aperitif that owes its flavours
and aromas to sweet and bitter oranges.

❶ INGREDIENTS

80 ML (2½ FL OZ) APEROL
100 ML (3½ FL OZ) PROSECCO
100 ML (3½ FL OZ) COCONUT BLOSSOM SYRUP
350 ML (12½ FL OZ) SODA WATER
1 ORANGE, THINLY SLICED

❷ EQUIPMENT

DIGITAL SCALES · MEASURING JUG · FREEZABLE CONTAINER · 8 CANAPÉ CUPS

❸ METHOD

In a jug, mix the Aperol, prosecco, coconut
blossom syrup and soda water. Divide
the mixture between the cups and freeze
for 5–6 hours or until firm. Remove from
the freezer and scrape the mixture into
flakes with a fork. Continue to freeze for
5–6 hours. Serve each cup with a slice of
orange to garnish.

EARL'S PUNCH

An elegant blend of Earl Grey tea and Cognac for discerning taste buds.

SERVES 8

Ingredients
500 ml (17 fl oz) brewed Earl Grey tea, cooled
100 ml (3½ fl oz) Martell VS Cognac
100 g (3½ oz) runny honey
100 ml (3½ fl oz) lemon juice
8 lemon slices

Equipment
measuring jug, digital scales,
8 popsicle moulds, 8 wooden popsicle sticks

Method
In a jug, mix the tea, Cognac, honey and lemon juice. Divide the mixture between the moulds, place the lid on the tray, and freeze for 30 minutes. Then add a lemon slice to each mould, slide the popsicle sticks into the lid slots and freeze for a further 12–14 hours, until solid.

PALOMA

Grapefruit, vanilla, tequila and lime marry perfectly in the Paloma.

SERVES 8

Ingredients
100 ml (3½ fl oz) tequila
500 ml (17 fl oz) pink grapefruit juice
100 ml (3½ fl oz) light agave syrup
2 teaspoons vanilla paste
½ pink grapefruit, thinly sliced into half moons

Equipment
measuring jug, digital scales,
8 popsicle moulds, 8 wooden popsicle sticks

Method
In a jug, mix the tequila, pink grapefruit juice, agave syrup and vanilla paste. Divide the mixture between popsicle moulds, place the lid on the tray, and freeze for 30 minutes. Then add the grapefruit slices to the moulds, slide the popsicle sticks into the lid slots and freeze for a further 12–14 hours, until solid.

6

SPRITZ
AND SPARKLE

Effervescent fun and a bit of bling is just what you need to add some magic to your party.

ELDERFLOWER & ROSÉ SPRITZ POPS

❶ INGREDIENTS

100 ML (3½ FL OZ) ELDERFLOWER LIQUEUR
150 ML (5 FL OZ) ROSÉ
60 ML (2 FL OZ) LIGHT AGAVE SYRUP
250 ML (8½ FL OZ) SPARKLING MINERAL WATER
8 STRAWBERRIES, HULLED AND SLICED IN 3

❷ EQUIPMENT

DIGITAL SCALES   MEASURING JUG   8 POPSICLE MOULDS & STICKS

❸ METHOD

SERVES 8
Gentle, elegant, floral and sparkly.

Mix the elderflower liqueur, rosé, agave syrup and water in a jug. Pour into the popsicle moulds. Slide 3 strawberry slices into each mould. Place the lid on the tray, and slide the popsicle sticks into the lid slots. Freeze for 12–14 hours, until solid.

MANGO GINGER FIZZ

SERVES 8
Tropical, fiery and fizzy – perfect for an afternoon pick-me-up.

❶ INGREDIENTS

400 G (14 OZ) MANGO, PEELED AND DESTONED
THUMB-SIZED PIECE GINGER, GRATED
60 ML (2 FL OZ) LIGHT AGAVE SYRUP
100 ML (3½ FL OZ) GIN • JUICE OF 1 LIME
330 ML (11 FL OZ) FIERY GINGER BEER

❷ EQUIPMENT

| BLENDER | DIGITAL SCALES | MEASURING JUG | 8 POPSICLE MOULDS & STICKS |

❸ METHOD

Blitz the mango, ginger, agave syrup, gin and lime juice in a blender or food processor until smooth. Pour into a jug, then mix in the ginger beer, divide the mixture between popsicle moulds and freeze for 30 minutes. Slide the popsicle sticks into the lid slots and continue to freeze for 12–14 hours, until solid.

GOLDEN POP

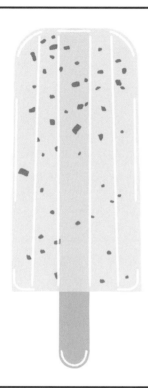

❶ INGREDIENTS

330 ML (11 FL OZ) FIERY GINGER BEER
120 ML (4 FL OZ) GOLD CINNAMON VODKA
(SUCH AS SMIRNOFF GOLD)
270 ML (9 FL OZ) CLEAR COLD-PRESSED APPLE JUICE
2 SHEETS EDIBLE GOLD LEAF OR
BRONZE SPRINKLES (OPTIONAL)

❷ EQUIPMENT

DIGITAL   MEASURING   8 POPSICLE
SCALES   JUG   MOULDS & STICKS

❸ METHOD

In a jug, mix the ginger beer, cinnamon vodka
and apple juice. Divide the mixture between
the popsicle moulds and freeze for
30 minutes. Then slide the popsicle sticks
into the lid slots and freeze for 12–14 hours,
until solid. Remove the pops from the moulds
and lightly dot with edible gold leaf or bronze
sprinkles, if desired.

SERVES 8
Bling up your pop with gold-leaf vodka!

RASPBERRY AÇAI SPRITZER

SERVES 8
Spritz yourself with this antioxidant-rich fruit pop. Açai is immune-stimulating and energy-boosting.

❶ INGREDIENTS

300 G (10½ OZ) RASPBERRIES
60 ML (2 FL OZ) VODKA
60 ML (2 FL OZ) CHAMBORD
1 BUNCH MINT, STALKS DISCARDED
4 TABLESPOONS AÇAI BERRY POWDER
400 ML (13½ FL OZ) CLUB SODA
8 CHERRIES, DESTONED AND HALVED

❷ EQUIPMENT

BLENDER   DIGITAL   MEASURING   8 POPSICLE
          SCALES   JUG   MOULDS & STICKS

❸ METHOD

In a blender or food processor, blitz the raspberries, vodka, Chambord, mint and açai until smooth and then pour into a jug. Add the club soda and mix well. Divide the mixture between the moulds and freeze for 30 minutes. Then add the cherries to each mould, slide the popsicle sticks into the lid slots and freeze for a further 12–14 hours, until solid.

CHAMPAGNE PASSION	❶ INGREDIENTS

200 ML (7 FL OZ) CHAMPAGNE
50 ML (1¾ FL OZ) COCONUT BLOSSOM SYRUP
350 ML (12 FL OZ) CLUB SODA
5 PASSION FRUITS, PULP SCOOPED

❷ EQUIPMENT

DIGITAL SCALES · MEASURING JUG · 8 POPSICLE MOULDS & STICKS

❸ METHOD

In a jug, mix the Champagne, coconut blossom syrup and club soda. Divide the passion fruit pulp between the popsicle moulds, and pour in the Champagne mixture. Place the lid on the tray and freeze for 30 minutes. Then slide the popsicle sticks into the lid slots and freeze for a further 12–14 hours, until solid.

SERVES 8
This combo is a real favourite! Sparkling and sweet, slightly sour, and fragrant with passion fruit.

HARD CIDER SPRITZ

High-quality apple cider is needed here (not the sweet stuff). Finished with whiskey and an apple wedge – perfect for autumn.

SERVES 8

Ingredients
200 ml (7 fl oz) cider
30 ml (1 fl oz) whiskey
juice of 1 lemon
400 ml (13½ fl oz) club soda
1 red apple, sliced into 8 thin wedges

Equipment
measuring jug, digital scales, 8 popsicle moulds, 8 wooden popsicle sticks

Method
In a jug, mix the cider, whiskey, lemon juice and club soda. Divide the mixture between the popsicle moulds, place the lid on the tray, and freeze for 30 minutes. Then add the apple slices, slide the popsicle sticks down into the lid slots and freeze for a further 12–14 hours, until solid.

AFTERGLOW

A delicious pop with blended melon, almond extract and lime, finished with a prosecco spritz.

SERVES 8

Ingredients
250 g (9 oz) melon pieces
2 teaspoons almond extract
60 g (2 oz) runny honey
300 ml (10 fl oz) prosecco
2 limes, 1 juiced and 1 thinly sliced

Equipment
blender or food processor, measuring jug, digital scales, large silicon ice-cube mould, plastic or wooden spoons

Method
In a blender or food processor, blitz the melon, almond extract and honey until smooth. Pour into a jug, add the prosecco and lime juice, and mix well. Pour the mixture into the silicon ice-cube mould, freeze for 30 minutes, then add a slice of lime and a spoon to each mould. Freeze for 12–14 hours, until solid.

7

LUXURIOUSLY
CREAMY

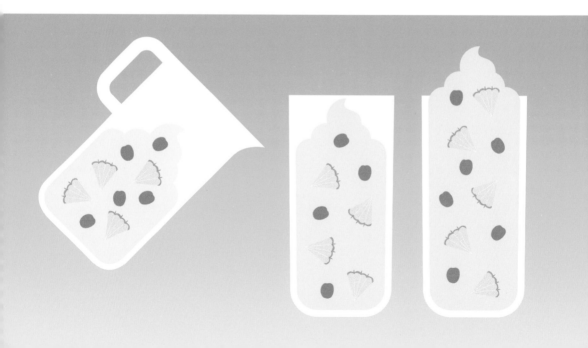

A lush marriage of ice lolly and booze in a pop. Creamy and decadent, they could easily pass for a dessert.

CHI CHI HAWAIIAN COCONUT POP

❶ INGREDIENTS

100 ML (3½ FL OZ) WHITE RUM
160 ML (5½ FL OZ) COCONUT CREAM
60 ML (2 FL OZ) LIGHT AGAVE SYRUP
500 G (1 LB 2 OZ) PINEAPPLE, PEELED AND CHOPPED
JUICE OF 1 LIME

❷ EQUIPMENT

BLENDER   DIGITAL SCALES   MEASURING JUG   8 POPSICLE MOULDS & STICKS

❸ METHOD

Blitz the rum, coconut cream, agave syrup, pineapple and lime juice in a blender or food processor until smooth. Divide the mixture between the popsicle moulds and freeze for 30 minutes. Then slide the popsicle sticks into the lid slots and freeze for 12–14 hours, until solid.

SERVES 8
The fresh pineapple, coconut cream, lime and rum in this pop transport you to the shores of Honolulu.

DIRTY BANANA COFFEE POP

50 ML (1¾ FL OZ) RUM
4 BANANAS, PEELED
60 ML (2 FL OZ) COFFEE LIQUEUR, SUCH AS KAHLÚA
160 G (5½ OZ) COCONUT CREAM

❷ EQUIPMENT

BLENDER   DIGITAL SCALES   MEASURING JUG   8 POPSICLE MOULDS & STICKS

❸ METHOD

Blitz the rum, bananas, coffee liqueur and coconut cream in a blender or food processor. Divide the mixture between the popsicle moulds, place the lid on the tray and freeze for 30 minutes. Slide in the popsicle sticks, then freeze for 12–14 hours, until solid.

SERVES 8
Creamy and light, yet slightly dirty.

ANGEL'S DELIGHT

SERVES 8

Not as frou-frou as it sounds. With its light pink colour, it certainly looks like something an angel might delight in.

❶ INGREDIENTS

50 ML (1¾ FL OZ) GIN
50 ML (1¾ FL OZ) GRAND MARNIER
50 ML (1¾ FL OZ) LIGHT AGAVE SYRUP
300 ML (10 FL OZ) SINGLE CREAM
200 ML (7 FL OZ) GREEK YOGHURT
8 DASHES SUGAR-FREE GRENADINE

❷ EQUIPMENT

DIGITAL SCALES   MEASURING JUG   8 POPSICLE MOULDS & STICKS

❸ METHOD

In a jug, mix the gin, Grand Marnier, agave syrup, cream and yoghurt. Place a dash of grenadine into each mould, then divide the creamy mixture between the moulds, making sure that you tap out any air bubbles. Place the lid on the tray and slide the popsicle sticks into the lid slots. Freeze for 12–14 hours, until solid.

GRASSHOPPER

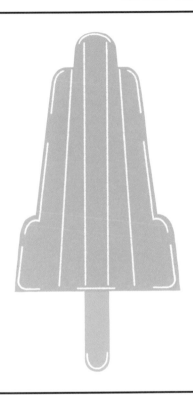

❶ INGREDIENTS

75 ML (2½ FL OZ) CRÈME DE MENTHE
25 ML (¾ FL OZ) VODKA
60 ML (2 FL OZ) LIGHT AGAVE SYRUP
350 ML (12 FL OZ) SINGLE CREAM
150 G (5 OZ) GREEK YOGHURT
1 BUNCH MINT, STALKS REMOVED
DASH MILK (IF NEEDED)

❷ EQUIPMENT

BLENDER   DIGITAL SCALES   MEASURING JUG   8 POPSICLE MOULDS & STICKS

❸ METHOD

In a blender or food processor, blitz the crème de menthe, vodka, agave syrup, cream, yoghurt and mint until creamy and a nice pale green. At this stage, if the mixture is too stiff, add a dash of milk. Divide the mixture between the moulds, put the lid on the tray and slide in the sticks. Freeze for 12–14 hours.

SERVES 8
A simple classic, which tastes like a mint milkshake. Adding yoghurt lightens the taste.

RASPY CRÈME

❶ INGREDIENTS

50 ML (1¾ FL OZ) CHAMBORD
100 ML (3½ FL OZ) LIGHT AGAVE SYRUP
300 G (10½ OZ) FRESH RASPBERRIES
300 ML (10 FL OZ) SINGLE CREAM
200 G (7 OZ) GREEK YOGHURT
50 ML (1¾ FL OZ) KAHLÚA

❷ EQUIPMENT

BLENDER   MEASURING   GLASS   8 POPSICLE
          JUG   BOWL   MOULDS & STICKS

❸ METHOD

In a blender or food processor, blitz the Chambord and 50 ml (1¾ fl oz) of the agave syrup with the raspberries to form a thick fruit purée, then pour into a jug and set aside. In a bowl, mix the remaining agave syrup, cream, Greek yoghurt and Kahlúa. Start by dividing a third of the fruit purée between the popsicle moulds, followed by a third of the cream mixture, alternating the layers until both mixtures have been used. Place the lid on the tray, and freeze for 30 minutes. Then slide the popsicle sticks into the lid slots and freeze for a further 12–14 hours.

SERVES 8
Rich flavours of cream and Kahlúa layered with fresh, tart raspberries and Chambord – this is perfect as a dessert for a crowd.

MUDSLIDE

❶ INGREDIENTS

1 TEASPOON INSTANT COFFEE GRANULES
100 ML (3½ FL OZ) HOT WATER
20 ML (¾ FL OZ) VODKA
40 ML (1¼ FL OZ) KAHLÚA
40 ML (1¼ FL OZ) IRISH CREAM LIQUEUR
250 ML (8½ FL OZ) SINGLE CREAM
50 ML (1¾ FL OZ) AGAVE SYRUP
150 G (5 OZ) GREEK YOGHURT

❷ EQUIPMENT

DIGITAL SCALES   MEASURING JUG   8 POPSICLE MOULDS & STICKS

❸ METHOD

Mix the instant coffee and hot water in a jug and leave to cool. Once cooled, add the vodka, Kahlúa, Irish cream liqueur, cream, agave syrup and Greek yoghurt. Mix well and divide the mixture between the popsicle moulds. Place the lid on the tray, and freeze for 30 minutes. Then slide the popsicle sticks into the lid slots and freeze for a further 12–14 hours, until solid.

SERVES 8
Creamy and boozy – how can you make a mudslide better? Put it on a stick!

KEY LIME

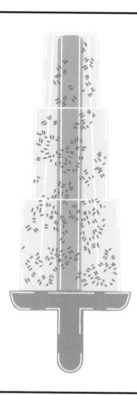

❶ INGREDIENTS

80 ML (2½ FL OZ) VODKA
100 ML (3½ FL OZ) LIGHT AGAVE SYRUP
ZEST AND JUICE OF 4 LIMES
300 ML (10 FL OZ) DOUBLE CREAM
200 G (7 OZ) GREEK YOGHURT

❷ EQUIPMENT

DIGITAL SCALES

MEASURING JUG

8 POPSICLE MOULDS & STICKS

❸ METHOD

In a jug, mix the vodka, agave syrup, lime juice, cream and Greek yoghurt. Divide the mixture between the popsicle moulds, place the lid on the tray, and freeze for 30 minutes. Then slide the popsicle sticks into the lid slots and freeze for a further 12–14 hours, until solid. Serve with the reserved lime zest scattered over the top.

SERVES 8
The ultimate pop – everything you want! Creamy, light, zingy and boozy – a pie on a stick.

PINK LADY

❶ INGREDIENTS

100 ML (3½ FL OZ) GIN
GRATED ZEST AND JUICE OF 1 LIME
JUICE OF 1 LEMON
20 ML (¾ FL OZ) SUGAR-FREE GRENADINE
200 G (7 OZ) FRESH OR FROZEN STRAWBERRIES
100 G (3½ OZ) FRESH OR FROZEN RASPBERRIES
150 G (5 OZ) GREEK YOGHURT
250 ML (8½ FL OZ) CLUB SODA

❷ EQUIPMENT

DIGITAL SCALES   MEASURING JUG   8 POPSICLE MOULDS & STICKS

❸ METHOD

In a blender or food processor, blitz the gin, lime and lemon juices, grenadine, strawberries, raspberries and yoghurt until smooth. Pour into a jug and top with the club soda. Divide the mixture between the popsicle moulds, tap out any air bubbles, place the lid on the tray, and freeze for 30 minutes. Then slide the popsicle sticks into the lid slots and freeze for a further 12–14 hours, until solid. Serve with the reserved lime zest scattered over the top.

SERVES 8
The Pink Lady is a classic gin-based cocktail with a long history. The grenadine, strawberries and raspberries give it its gorgeous hue.

WHITE RUSSIAN

❶ INGREDIENTS

50 ML (1¾ FL OZ) VODKA • 50 ML (1¾ FL OZ) KAHLÚA
300 ML (10 FL OZ) DOUBLE (HEAVY) CREAM
200 G (7 OZ) GREEK YOGHURT
50 G (1¾ OZ) RUNNY HONEY

❷ EQUIPMENT

DIGITAL SCALES   MEASURING JUG   8 POPSICLE MOULDS & STICKS

❸ METHOD

In a jug, mix the vodka, Kahlúa, cream, yoghurt and honey until smooth. Divide the mixture between the popsicle moulds, making sure that you tap out any air bubbles, place the lid on the tray, and freeze for 30 minutes. Then slide the popsicle sticks into the lid slots and freeze for a further 12–14 hours, until solid.

SERVES 8
An easy-licking blend of vodka, coffee liqueur and cream, the White Russian was a favourite during the glory days of disco.

PINA COLADA

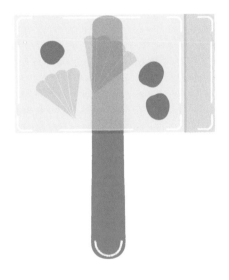

SERVES 6

A tropical blend of rich coconut, white rum and tangy pineapple topped with a Maraschino cherry – all that's missing is the sand between your toes.

❶ INGREDIENTS

400 G (14 OZ) FRESH PINEAPPLE, CUT INTO CHUNKS, RESERVING SOME FOR GARNISH
JUICE OF 1 LIME • 80 ML (2½ FL OZ) WHITE RUM
40 ML (1½ FL OZ) MALIBU • 1 × 400 ML (14 FL OZ) TIN COCONUT MILK • 6 MARASCHINO CHERRIES

❷ EQUIPMENT

LARGE SILICON
ICE-CUBE MOULDS

BLENDER DIGITAL SCALES MEASURING JUG 6 POPSICLE STICKS

❸ METHOD

In a food processor or blender, blitz the pineapple, lime juice, rum, Malibu and coconut milk until smooth. Pour the mixture into the ice-cube moulds and freeze for 30 minutes. Then add the Maraschino cherries and reserved pineapple pieces to each section and freeze for a further 12–14 hours, until solid.

CLASSICS
WITH A TWIST

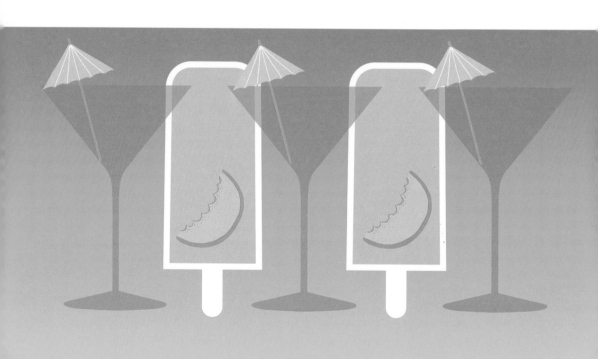

Breathe new life into old cocktails.
These frozen pops offer a modern twist on
the classics.

STRAWBERRY ROSE DAIQUIRI

SERVES 8
The sweetness of strawberries and the kick of lime make this classic daiquiri a real crowd pleaser, with a twist of rose water and pink lemonade.

❶ INGREDIENTS

400 G (14 OZ) STRAWBERRIES, HULLED
1 TABLESPOON ROSE WATER
1 TEASPOON VANILLA EXTRACT
275 ML (9½ FL OZ) PINK LEMONADE
100 ML (3½ FL OZ) WHITE RUM
JUICE OF 2 LIMES

❷ EQUIPMENT

BLENDER   DIGITAL SCALES   MEASURING JUG   8 POPSICLE MOULDS & STICKS

❸ METHOD

Blitz the strawberries, rose water, vanilla extract, pink lemonade, white rum and lime juice in a blender or food processor until smooth, then transfer to a jug and mix. Pour the mixture into the popsicle moulds, place the lid on the tray, and slide the popsicle sticks into the lid slots. Freeze for 12–14 hours, until solid.

ORANGE PEACH NEGRONI

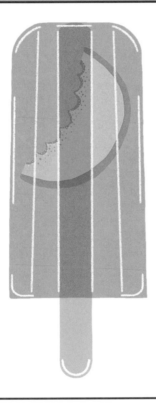

SERVES 8
The classic Negroni, garnished with
a slice of peach, on a stick.

❶ INGREDIENTS

400 ML (13½ FL OZ) SMOOTH ORANGE JUICE
100 ML (3½ FL OZ) COCONUT BLOSSOM SYRUP
OR LIGHT AGAVE SYRUP
50 ML (1¾ FL OZ) CAMPARI
30 ML (1 FL OZ) VERMOUTH
20 ML (¾ FL OZ) GIN
1 PEACH, SLICED INTO THIN WEDGES

❷ EQUIPMENT

DIGITAL
SCALES

MEASURING
JUG

8 POPSICLE
MOULDS & STICKS

❸ METHOD

In a jug, mix the orange juice and coconut
blossom syrup. If you find the syrup a little
thick, gently heat in a microwave for
2–3 minutes. Stir in the Campari, Vermouth
and gin. Pour the mixture into the moulds
and freeze for 30 minutes. Place the lid on
the tray, slide the peach slices onto the
sticks, and insert the sticks into the lid
slots. Freeze for 12–14 hours, until solid.

COSMOPOLITAN POPS

Carrie's favourite cocktail – but here even better in its frozen form. Make like a Manhattan socialite!

SERVES 8

❶ INGREDIENTS

500 ml (17 fl oz) cranberry juice

60 ml (2 fl oz) Cointreau

40 ml (1¼ fl oz) vodka

60 ml (2 fl oz) light agave syrup

juice of 1 lime

1 orange, thinly sliced

❷ EQUIPMENT
measuring jug
digital scales
8 popsicle moulds
8 popsicle sticks

❸ METHOD
In a jug, mix the cranberry juice, Cointreau, vodka, agave syrup and lime juice. Divide the mixture between the popsicle moulds and freeze for 30 minutes. Then slide a few orange slices into each mould, place the lid on the tray, and insert the popsicle sticks into the lid slots. Freeze for a further 12–14 hours, until solid.

BLUE LAGOON

Enjoy this version of the classic 1970s cocktail – a delicious, vibrantly blue pop.

SERVES 8

❶ INGREDIENTS

500 ml (17 fl oz) sugar-free lemonade

40 ml (1½ fl oz) vodka

60 ml (2 fl oz) curaçao

❷ EQUIPMENT
measuring jug
digital scales
8 popsicle moulds
8 popsicle sticks

❸ METHOD
In a glass jug, mix the lemonade, vodka and curaçao. Divide the mixture between popsicle moulds and freeze for 30 minutes. Slide the popsicle sticks into the lid slots and freeze for 12–14 hours, until solid.

JAPANESE SLIPPER

Treat your guests with this cherry-topped pop, frozen and served in cups.

SERVES 8

❶ INGREDIENTS

60 ml (2 fl oz) Midori

40 ml (1¼ fl oz) Cointreau

550 ml (19 fl oz) sugar-free lemonade

6 Maraschino cherries, with stems

❷ EQUIPMENT
measuring jug
digital scales
8 wooden canapé cups

❸ METHOD
In a glass jug, mix the Midori, Contreau and the lemonade. Divide the mixture between the cups and freeze for 30 minutes. Then add the cherries, making sure that the stems are hanging out, and freeze for a further 12–14 hours, until solid. Serve in the cups with spoons.

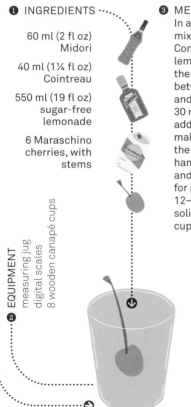

WHITE PEACH BELLINI

White peaches and Champagne are blitzed to create a delicate classic.

SERVES 8

❶ INGREDIENTS

350 g (12½ oz) white-fleshed peaches (about 4), peeled and destoned

200 ml (7 fl oz) Champagne

light agave syrup (optional)

❷ EQUIPMENT
blender or food processor
measuring jug
digital scales
8 popsicle moulds
8 wooden popsicle sticks

❸ METHOD
Place the peach in a blender or food processor and blitz until smooth. Taste, then add some agave syrup if desired. Place the mixture in a glass jug and add the Champagne. Divide the mixture between the moulds, place the lid on the tray, and freeze for 30 minutes. Slide the popsicle sticks down into the lid slots and freeze for a further 12–14 hours, until solid.

SPIKED ESPRESSO SHAVED ICE	❶ INGREDIENTS

10 ML (¼ FL OZ) VODKA
500 ML (17 FL OZ) COFFEE, COOLED
80 ML (2½ FL OZ) COFFEE LIQUEUR, SUCH AS KAHLÚA
50 ML (1¾ FL OZ) COCONUT BLOSSOM NECTAR
1 TEASPOON GOOD-QUALITY COCOA POWDER,
TO SERVE

❷ EQUIPMENT

CAFETIERE   DIGITAL SCALES   MEASURING JUG   MEASURING SPOONS

8 MINI LOAF CASES   FORK

❸ METHOD

SERVES 8
A very grown-up way to have shaved ice! For a summer dinner party, serve this ice instead of an espresso at the end of a meal.

In a jug, mix together all the ingredients, except the cocoa powder. Divide the mixture between the loaf cases and freeze for 5–6 hours, or until firm. Remove from the freezer and use a fork to scrape the mixture into flakes. Serve in bowls, dusted with cocoa powder.

PASSION FRUIT CAIPIROSKA

A tropical island pop.

SERVES 8

Ingredients
100 ml (3½ fl oz) vodka
50 ml (1¾ fl oz) coconut blossom syrup
2 limes, 1 juiced and 1 sliced into thin rounds
8 mint leaves
8 passion fruits, halved, pulp and seeds reserved
400 ml (13½ fl oz) club soda

Equipment
measuring jug, digital scales, 8 popsicle moulds,
8 popsicle sticks

Method
In a jug, mix the vodka, coconut blossom syrup,
lime juice and club soda. Place a slice of lime and
a mint leaf into each of the moulds. Divide the
mixture between moulds, place the lid on the tray
and freeze for 30 minutes before sliding in the
popsicle sticks. Freeze for a further 12–14 hours,
until solid.

SEX ON THE BEACH

Enjoy this deliciously provocative pop.

SERVES 8

Ingredients
20 ml (¾ fl oz) vodka
20 ml (¾ fl oz) peach schnapps
200 ml (7 fl oz) orange juice
40 ml (1¼ fl oz) Chambord
200 ml (7 fl oz) cranberry juice

Equipment
2 jugs, digital scales, 8 popsicle moulds,
8 popsicle sticks

Method
In a jug, mix the vodka, peach schnapps and
orange juice, and store in the fridge. In another
jug, mix the Chambord and cranberry juice. Divide
half of the red mixture between the moulds, and
freeze for 12 hours. Store the remaining mixture in
the fridge. The next day, divide the orange mixture
between the moulds, then freeze for another
12 hours. Top with the red mixture, add the sticks
and freeze for a further 12 hours, until solid.

MIMOSA POP

Serve these at your next brunch get-together. Simple, yet always impressive.

SERVES 8

Ingredients
400 ml (13½ fl oz) smooth orange juice
200 ml (7 fl oz) Champagne
light agave syrup (optional)
1 orange, thinly sliced

Equipment
glass measuring jug, digital scales,
8 popsicle moulds, 8 popsicle sticks

Method
In a jug, mix the orange juice and Champagne together. Taste and add some agave syrup if desired. Divide the mixture between the moulds, place the lid on the tray and freeze for 30 minutes. Then slide the slices of orange down the sides of the moulds before inserting the sticks, and freeze for a further 12–14 hours.

JELLY FISH

If you want to make a pop that's sure to get people talking, this is one that most people have never tried but everyone will be curious about!

SERVES 8

Ingredients
30 ml (1 fl oz) vodka
70 ml (2¼ fl oz) blue Curaçao
60 ml (2 fl oz) light agave syrup
500 ml (17 fl oz) club soda
200 g (7 oz) freshly whipped cream

Equipment
2 jugs, digital scales, 8 popsicle moulds,
8 popsicle sticks

Method
In a jug, mix the vodka, blue Curaçao, agave syrup and club soda. Divide the mixture between the popsicle moulds, place the lid on the tray, and freeze for 1 hour. Top with the whipped cream. Slide the popsicle sticks into the lid slots and continue to freeze for a further 12–14 hours, until solid.

KIR ROYALE

Summer drinking trends may come and go, but the kir royale is an eternal favourite.

SERVES 8

Ingredients
30 ml (1 fl oz) crème de cassis
200 ml (7 fl oz) Champagne
350 ml (12 fl oz) club soda
50 ml (1¾ fl oz) light agave syrup

Equipment
glass measuring jug, digital scales,
8 popsicle moulds, 8 popsicle sticks

Method
Mix the crème de cassis, Champagne, club soda and agave syrup in a jug. Divide the mixture between popsicle moulds, place the lid on the tray, and freeze for 30 minutes. Then slide the popsicle sticks into the lid slots and freeze for a further 12–14 hours, until solid.

VODKA RED BULL

Reminiscent of student days!

SERVES 6

Ingredients
500 ml (17 fl oz) sugar-free Red Bull
80 ml (2½ fl oz) vodka

Equipment
glass measuring jug, digital scales,
6 popsicle moulds, 6 popsicle sticks

Method
In a jug, mix the Red Bull and vodka. Divide the mixture between the popsicle moulds, place the lid on the tray, and freeze for 30 minutes. Then slide the popsicle sticks into the lid slots and freeze for a further 12–14 hours, until solid.

VODKA SUNSET

Simplicity on a stick, with a blend of blood orange and vodka – perfect for any evening!

SERVES 8

Ingredients
100 ml (3½ fl oz) vodka
150 ml (5 fl oz) orange juice
150 ml (5 fl oz) blood orange juice
dash of Chambord
250 ml (8½ fl oz) club soda

Equipment
measuring jug, digital scales,
8 popsicle moulds, 8 popsicle sticks

Method
In a jug, mix the vodka, orange and blood orange juices with a dash of Chambord and the club soda. Divide the mixture between the popsicle moulds, place the lid on the tray, and freeze for 30 minutes. Then slide the popsicle sticks into the lid slots and continue to freeze for a further 12–14 hours, until solid.

RUM 'N' COKE

Classic and always a crowd pleaser, with no added sugar!

SERVES 8

Ingredients
500 ml (17 fl oz) sugar-free cola
100 ml (3½ fl oz) dark rum

Equipment
measuring jug, digital scales,
8 popsicle moulds, 8 popsicle sticks

Method
In a jug, mix the cola and rum. Divide the mixture between the popsicle moulds, place the lid on the tray, and freeze for 30 minutes. Then slide the popsicle sticks into the lid slots and freeze for a further 12–14 hours, until solid.

WHISKEY 'N' SODA

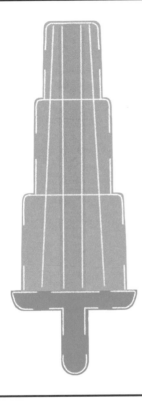

SERVES 8
The classic addition of soda enhances the flavours of the whiskey. Why not take it one step further and freeze?

❶ INGREDIENTS

100 ML (3½ FL OZ) WHISKEY
70 G (2½ OZ) RUNNY HONEY
500 ML (17 FL OZ) CLUB SODA

❷ EQUIPMENT

DIGITAL SCALES   MEASURING JUG   8 POPSICLE MOULDS & STICKS

❸ METHOD

In a jug, mix the whiskey, honey and club soda. Divide the mixture between the popsicle moulds, place the lid on the tray, and freeze for 30 minutes. Then slide the popsicle sticks into the lid slots and freeze for a further 12–14 hours, until solid.

SPICE

As the weather turns colder, spice up your pops with rich, warming flavours in frozen form.

DIRTY MANGO LASSI

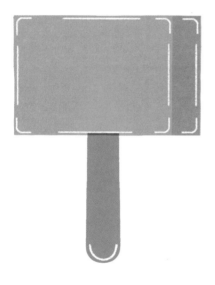

3 MANGOES, PEELED, DESTONED AND CHOPPED
1 TSP GROUND CARDAMOM
300 G (10½ OZ) GREEK YOGHURT
100 ML (3½ FL OZ) DARK AGAVE SYRUP
100 ML (3½ FL OZ) DARK RUM
ZEST AND JUICE OF 2 LIMES

❷ EQUIPMENT

6 PLASTIC
SPOONS

BLENDER   MEASURING   LARGE SILICON
JUG   ICE-CUBE MOULDS

❸ METHOD

SERVES 8
It's dirty because it's spiked – however, it's
naughty and nice as the whole mango is
used and blended with cardamom and rum.

Blitz the mangoes with the cardamom seeds,
Greek yoghurt, agave syrup, rum, lime juice
and zest in a food processor or blender. Pour
into the ice-cube moulds and place in the
freezer for 1½ hours. Remove from the freezer
and insert the spoons into the centre of each
mould. Return to the freezer for 12–14 hours.

COLD TODDY

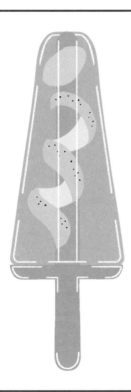

SERVES 6
Essentially a hot toddy, frozen. It's best to allow the spices to infuse for as long as possible for maximum flavour.

❶ INGREDIENTS

500 ML (17 FL OZ) WATER
30 G (1 OZ) HONEY • 10 CLOVES • 2 CINNAMON STICKS
1 CM (½ IN) PIECE OF GINGER, PEELED AND SLICED LENGTHWAYS INTO 8
JUICE OF 1 LEMON • 8 STRIPS OF LEMON PEEL
GRATING OF NUTMEG
100 ML (3½ FL OZ) WHISKEY

❷ EQUIPMENT

DIGITAL SCALES   MEASURING JUG   8 POPSICLE MOULDS & STICKS

❸ METHOD

Place all the ingredients, except the whiskey, into a pan over a medium heat and bring to the boil. Leave to infuse. Once cooled, add the whiskey. Remove the lemon peel and ginger and place one of each into the moulds with a grating of nutmeg. Discard the other items and divide the liquid between the moulds. Freeze for 30 minutes. Then slide in the sticks and freeze for a further 12–14 hours.

MIXED BERRY MAPLE SPICE

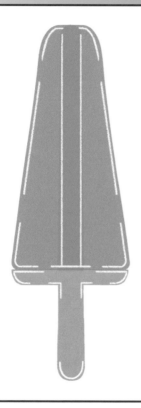

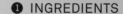

300 G (10½ OZ) MIXED BERRIES
100 ML (3½ FL OZ) MAPLE SYRUP
8 BLACK PEPPERCORNS
PEEL AND JUICE OF 1 LEMON
200 ML (7 FL OZ) FIERY GINGER BEER
FRESHLY CRACKED PEPPER, TO GARNISH

② EQUIPMENT

BLENDER DIGITAL SCALES MEASURING JUG 8 POPSICLE MOULDS & STICKS

③ METHOD

In a blender or food processor, blitz the berries, maple syrup, peppercorns and lemon juice until smooth. Pour into a jug and add the ginger beer. Divide the mixture between the popsicle moulds, place the lid on the tray, and freeze for 30 minutes. Then add the lemon peel, slide the popsicle sticks nto the lid slots and freeze for a further 12–14 hours, until solid. Serve with a few grinds of black pepper.

SERVES 8
This fiery pop will spice up any event.

CRANBERRY CINNAMON

A spiced cranberry poptail served on a cinnamon stick – a nice little gift.

SERVES 8

Ingredients
600 ml (20½ fl oz) cranberry juice
100 ml (3½ fl oz) white rum
100 ml (3½ fl oz) agave syrup
2 teaspoons ground cinnamon
8 strips of orange peel
8 cinnamon sticks (optional)

Equipment
measuring jug, digital scales, 8 popsicle moulds, 8 popsicle sticks

Method
In a jug, mix the cranberry juice, rum, agave syrup and ground cinnamon. Divide the mixture between the moulds, place the lid on the tray, and freeze for 30 minutes. Add the strips of zest before sliding the popsicle sticks (or cinnamon sticks) into the lid slots. Freeze for a further 12–14 hours, until solid.

BLOODY MARY

The classic hangover cure with a little extra zing.

SERVES 8

Ingredients
100 ml (3½ fl oz) vodka
500 ml (17 fl oz) tomato juice
juice of 1 lemon
8 dashes Worcestershire sauce
8 dashes Tabasco (hot pepper sauce)
pinch of celery salt
pinch of freshly ground black pepper
8 small celery stalks, with leaves

Equipment
measuring jug, digital scales, 8 popsicle moulds, 8 popsicle sticks

Method
Place all of the ingredients, except the celery, into a large jug and mix well. Place the celery sticks in the moulds. Divide the tomato mixture between moulds, place the lid on the tray, and freeze for 30 minutes. Then slide the sticks into the slots and freeze for a further 12–14 hours.

DAY TRIPPER

❶ INGREDIENTS

500 ML (17 FL OZ) BREWED BLACK TEA
100 ML (3½ FL OZ) GINGER SYRUP (SEE RECIPE ON
PAGE 31), PLUS 8 SLICES OF GINGER FROM THE SYRUP
100 ML (3½ FL OZ) VODKA
2 LEMONS, 1 JUICED, 1 SLICED
3 TEASPOONS DRIED LAVENDER

❷ EQUIPMENT

DIGITAL   MEASURING   8 POPSICLE
SCALES   JUG   MOULDS & STICKS

❸ METHOD

In a jug, mix the black tea, ginger syrup,
vodka and lemon juice. Place a lemon slice,
a piece of ginger and a pinch of lavender into
each popsicle mould. Divide the tea mixture
between the moulds, place the lid on the tray
and slide the popsicle sticks into the lid slots.
Freeze for 12–14 hours, until solid.

SERVES 8
Reminiscent of an iced tea, but infused
with ginger and lavender.

FRESH GINGER MOSCOW MULE

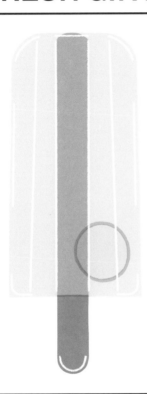

SERVES 8
The ginger gives this Moscow mule an extra kick.

❶ INGREDIENTS

100 ML (3½ FL OZ) VODKA
JUICE OF 1 LIME
1 THUMB-SIZED PIECE GINGER, PEELED AND GRATED
60 ML (2 FL OZ) GINGER SYRUP (SEE RECIPE ON PAGE 31),
PLUS 8 PIECES OF GINGER FROM THE SYRUP
400 ML (13½ FL OZ) CLUB SODA

❷ EQUIPMENT

DIGITAL SCALES   MEASURING JUG   8 POPSICLE MOULDS & STICKS

❸ METHOD

In a jug, mix the vodka, lime juice, grated ginger, ginger syrup and club soda. Divide the mixture between the popsicle moulds, place the lid on the tray, and freeze for 30 minutes. Then add the ginger pieces from the syrup to the moulds, slide the popsicle sticks into the lid slots and freeze for a further 12–14 hours, until solid.

TONGUE
TEASERS

With a blend of exotic flavours and spices, these pops will tantalise your tongue with something different.

BEE STING

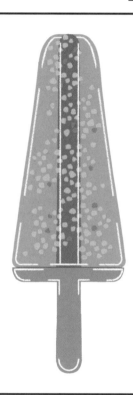

❶ INGREDIENTS

60 G (2 OZ) RUNNY HONEY, PLUS EXTRA TO SERVE
50 ML (1¾ FL OZ) WHISKEY • 50 ML (1¾ FL OZ) TEQUILA
250 ML (8½ FL OZ) CLEAR APPLE JUICE
250 ML (8½ FL OZ) FIERY GINGER BEER
8 TEASPOONS BEE POLLEN, PLUS EXTRA TO SERVE

❷ EQUIPMENT

DIGITAL SCALES   MEASURING JUG   8 POPSICLE MOULDS & STICKS

❸ METHOD

In a jug, mix the honey, whiskey, tequila, apple juice and ginger beer. Place a teaspoon of bee pollen in each of the moulds and divide the mixture between them. Place the lid on the tray and freeze for 30 minutes. Then slide the popsicle sticks into the lid slots and freeze for a further 12–14 hours, until solid. Serve with an extra drizzle of runny honey and bee pollen.

SERVES 8
This is a surprising pop: its bright hue, tangy-sweet taste and garnish of honey and bee pollen make it a deliciously decadent treat.

OUZO, LEMON & DILL POP

SERVES 8
Like a Greek summer holiday, this ouzo and fennel pop has a zesty, clean finish.

❶ INGREDIENTS

500 ML (17 FL OZ) CLOUDY
SUGAR-FREE LEMONADE
100 ML (3½ FL OZ) OUZO
50 ML (1¾ FL OZ) LIGHT AGAVE SYRUP
8 DILL SPRIGS

❷ EQUIPMENT

DIGITAL   MEASURING   8 POPSICLE
SCALES   JUG   MOULDS & STICKS

❸ METHOD

In a jug, mix the lemonade, ouzo and agave syrup together. Place a dill sprig in each popsicle mould and then divide the mixture between the moulds. Place the lid on the tray, and freeze for 30 minutes. Then slide the popsicle sticks into the lid slots and freeze for a further 12–14 hours, until solid.

FIRECRACKER SHAVED ICE

❶ INGREDIENTS

50 ML (1¾ FL OZ) VODKA • 50 ML (1¾ FL OZ) COINTREAU
JUICE OF ½ LIME • 50 ML (1¾ FL OZ) LIGHT AGAVE SYRUP
500 G (1 LB 2 OZ) WATERMELON, DESEEDED AND CUBED
1 TEASPOON CAYENNE PEPPER, PLUS EXTRA TO FINISH

❷ EQUIPMENT

8 WOODEN SPOONS   FORK

BLENDER   DIGITAL   MEASURING   8 CANAPÉ
           SCALES   JUG   CUPS

❸ METHOD

In a blender or food processor, blitz the
vodka, Cointreau, lime juice, agave syrup,
watermelon and cayenne. Divide the mixture
between the cups and freeze for 5–6 hours, or
until firm. Remove from the freezer and use a
fork to scrape the mixture into flakes.
Serve with spoons and sprinkled with
cayenne pepper.

SERVES 8
With the perfect balance of cool
watermelon and hot cayenne, this boozy
little firecracker will enliven your senses.

FROST BITE

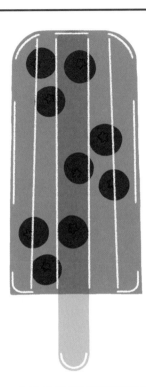

❶ INGREDIENTS

50 ML (1¾ FL OZ) BLUE CURAÇAO
60 ML (2 FL OZ) VODKA
600 ML (20½ FL OZ) PINEAPPLE JUICE
50 ML (1¾ FL OZ) LIGHT AGAVE SYRUP
100 G (3½ OZ) BLUEBERRIES

❷ EQUIPMENT

DIGITAL   MEASURING   8 POPSICLE
SCALES   JUG   MOULDS & STICKS

❸ METHOD

In a jug, mix the Curaçao, vodka, pineapple juice and agave syrup. Divide the mixture between the popsicle moulds, place the lid on the tray, and freeze for 30 minutes. Then add the blueberries, slide the popsicle sticks into the lid slots and freeze for a further 12–14 hours, until solid.

SERVES 8-10
It's impossible to have the blues when you're eating one of these yummy pops.

KALE POPTINI

A sweet, earthy superfood poptail.

SERVES 8

Ingredients
100 ml (3½ fl oz) vodka
2 cucumbers, roughly chopped
200 g (7 oz) frozen smoothie mix
   (such as mango or melon)
1 lemon, peeled
1 large handful kale, plus extra to garnish
1 bunch mint, plus extra to garnish

Equipment
blender or food processor, jug,
digital scales, large silicon ice-cube moulds,
8 wooden or plastic spoons

Method
In a blender, blitz all the ingredients until smooth.
Pour the mixture into the ice-cube moulds, and
place a kale piece in each section. Freeze for
30 minutes, then insert a spoon into each pop and
return to the freezer for up to 12 hours, until solid.

CHIA FRESCA POP

Chia fresca is a favourite in Central America.
Spiking it and freezing it really makes it pop.

SERVES 8

Ingredients
60 ml (2 fl oz) tequila
60 ml (2 fl oz) Aperol
600 ml (20½ fl oz) pineapple juice
juice of 1 lime
100 ml (3½ fl oz) light agave syrup
80 g (2¾ oz) chia seeds

Equipment
measuring jug, digital scales, 8 popsicle moulds,
8 popsicle sticks

Method
In a jug, mix the tequila, Aperol, pineapple and
lime juices with the agave syrup and chia seeds.
Allow to stand for 3 hours until the mixture
thickens. Divide the mixture between the moulds,
place the lid on the tray, and slide the sticks into
the slots. Freeze for 12–14 hours, until solid.

RATTLESNAKE

A pop with a bit of bite.

SERVES 8

Ingredients
100 ml (3½ fl oz) whiskey
100 ml (3½ fl oz) dark agave syrup
100 ml (3½ fl oz) egg whites* (about 4 eggs)
500 ml (17 fl oz) cloudy lemonade

Equipment
blender or food processor, glass measuring jug,
digital scales, 8 popsicle moulds,
8 popsicle sticks

Method
In a blender or food processor, blitz the whiskey
with the agave syrup and egg whites until fluffy.
Pour into a jug and let it sit for 30 minutes.
The mixture will start to separate, which causes
the snakeskin effect. Divide the mixture between
the moulds, place the lid on the tray, and slide
the sticks into the slots. Freeze for 12–14 hours,
until solid.

* NOTE: Raw egg is not recommended for the elderly, pregnant women,
children under the age of 4, and people with weakened immune systems.

AVOCADO MARGARITA

Light and creamy! Add jalapeño for an extra kick.

SERVES 12

Ingredients
2 avocados, destoned and peeled
100 ml (3½ fl oz) tequila
juice of 2 limes
1 handful coriander (cilantro), reserving a few
   leaves to garnish
100 ml (3½ fl oz) light agave syrup
300 ml (10 fl oz) soda water

Equipment
blender or food processor, measuring jug, digital
scales, 12-hole cupcake tray, 12 wooden sticks

Method
In a blender, blitz the avocados, tequila, lime
juice, coriander and agave syrup until smooth and
velvety. In a jug, combine the avocado mixture
with the soda water and mix well. Divide the
mixture between the holes of the tray, top with a
coriander leaf and freeze for 2–3 hours. Add the
sticks, then freeze for 12–14 hours, until solid.

LAVA FLOW SLUSHIE

SERVES 8

The combination of flavours in this slushie is amazing. Pineapple, coconut, strawberry and blood orange become a magically delicious pop.

❶ INGREDIENTS

60 ML (2 FL OZ/¼ CUP) MALIBU
40 ML (1¼ FL OZ) WHITE RUM
200 G (7 OZ) STRAWBERRIES,
HULLED AND ROUGHLY CHOPPED
250 ML (8½ FL OZ/1 CUP) COCONUT MILK
100 ML (3½ FL OZ) PINEAPPLE JUICE
200 ML (7 FL OZ) BLOOD ORANGE JUICE

❷ EQUIPMENT

2 FREEZABLE PLASTIC CONTAINERS

BLENDER   DIGITAL   MEASURING   8 SMALL
          SCALES   JUG   CUPS

❸ METHOD

In a blender or food processor, blitz all the ingredients, except the blood orange juice, until smooth. Place the mixture in a freezable plastic container and freeze for 5–6 hours. Remove from the freezer and use a fork to scrape the mixture into flakes. Then return the mixture to the freezer for a further 5 hours. Meanwhile, pour the blood orange juice into a freezable plastic container and freeze for 5–6 hours. Remove from the freezer and scrape the mixture into flakes. Return the mixture to the freezer for a further 5 hours. To serve, divide the strawberry mixture between small cups and top with the blood orange mixture.

THE GREEN GODDESS

Green goodness to nourish your inner goddess.

SERVES 8

Ingredients
100 ml (3½ fl oz) vodka
400 ml (13½ fl oz) brewed green tea
60 ml (2 fl oz) light agave syrup
1 cucumber, peeled and roughly chopped
1 jalapeño, thinly sliced
juice of 1 lemon
1 handful mint, stalks removed,
  plus 8 mint stalks to garnish

Equipment
blender or food processor, digital scales,
8 popsicle moulds, 8 popsicle sticks

Method
In a blender or food processor, blitz all of the
ingredients, except the mint stalks, until smooth.
Divide the mixture between the moulds and
freeze for 30 minutes. Then add the mint stalks,
slide in the sticks and freeze for a further
12–14 hours, until solid.

BLACK STRAP

An earthy poptail with a hint of delicious sourness
from the pomegranate.

SERVES 8

Ingredients
60 ml (2 fl oz) pomegranate molasses
100 ml (3½ fl oz) dark Jamaican rum
8 dashes of bitters
100 ml (3½ fl oz) dark agave syrup
500 ml (17 fl oz) fiery ginger beer
juice of 1 lime

Equipment
measuring jug, digital scales,
8 popsicle moulds, 8 popsicle sticks

Method
In a jug, mix the pomegranate molasses, rum,
bitters, agave syrup, ginger beer and lime juice.
Divide the mixture between the popsicle moulds,
place the lid on the tray, and freeze for
30 minutes. Then slide the popsicle sticks
into the lid slots and freeze for a further
12–14 hours, until solid.

EL NIÑO

❶ INGREDIENTS

JUICE OF 2 LIMES
100 ML (3½ FL OZ) TEQUILA
1 CUCUMBER, ROUGHLY CHOPPED
1 HANDFUL CORIANDER (CILANTRO)
100 ML (3½ FL OZ) LIGHT AGAVE SYRUP
300 ML (10 FL OZ) CLUB SODA
3 JALAPEÑOS, HALVED LENGTHWAYS

❷ EQUIPMENT

6 PLASTIC OR
WOOODEN SPOONS

BLENDER   DIGITAL   MEASURING   LARGE SILICON
           SCALES   JUG   ICE-CUBE MOULDS

❸ METHOD

SERVES 8
A cool and refreshing pop with a hot jalapeño tingle.

In a blender or food processor, blitz all the ingredients, except the jalapeños, until smooth, then pour into a jug. Stir in the club soda. Divide the mixture between the ice-cube moulds, freeze for 30 minutes. Then add a jalapeño half and spoon to each mould and freeze for a further 12–14 hours, until solid.

BALTIC BLACKCURRANT

Perfectly simple and berry delicious.

SERVES 8

Ingredients
70 ml (2½ fl oz) blackcurrant liqueur
30 ml (1 fl oz) vodka
500 ml (17 fl oz) sugar-free lemonade

Equipment
measuring jug, digital scales,
8 popsicle moulds, 8 popsicle sticks

Method
In a jug, mix the blackcurrant liqueur, vodka
and lemonade. Divide the mixture between the
popsicle moulds, place the lid on the tray, and
freeze for 30 minutes. Then slide the popsicle
sticks into the lid slots and freeze for a further
12–14 hours, until solid.

WOO WOO POP

A sweet and fruity classic pop, with the addition
of bitters to tantalise your taste buds.

SERVES 8

Ingredients
70 ml (2¼ fl oz) peach schnapps
30 ml (1 fl oz) vodka
dash of bitters
500 ml (17 fl oz) cranberry juice

Equipment
glass measuring jug, digital scales,
8 popsicle moulds, 8 popsicle sticks

Method
In a jug, mix the peach schnapps with the vodka,
bitters and cranberry juice. Divide the mixture
between the popsicle moulds, place the lid on
the tray, and freeze for 30 minutes. Then slide the
popsicle sticks into the lid slots and freeze for a
further 12–14 hours, until solid.

BOTANICAL

These plant-powered pops blend flowers and herbs. Fresh and aromatic, they will help you make the most of your garden.

MINT ELIXIR

❶ INGREDIENTS

2 LARGE HANDFULS MINT, STALKS REMOVED, CHOPPED
500 ML (17 FL OZ) CLUB SODA
100 ML (3½ FL OZ) GREEN CHARTREUSE
100 ML (3½ FL OZ) LIGHT AGAVE SYRUP
JUICE OF 1 LIME

❷ EQUIPMENT

DIGITAL SCALES   MEASURING JUG   8 POPSICLE MOULDS & STICKS

❸ METHOD

In a jug, mix all of the ingredients together. Divide the mixture between the popsicle moulds and freeze for 30 minutes. Then slide the popsicle sticks into the lid slots and freeze for 12–14 hours, until solid.

SERVES 8
There's no skimping on flavour in this iced mint potion.

FLORAL GIN & TONIC

❶ INGREDIENTS

100 ML (3½ FL OZ) GIN
500 ML (17 FL OZ) TONIC WATER
40 ML (1½ FL OZ) ORANGE BLOSSOM WATER
50 G (2 OZ) EDIBLE FLOWERS
½ ORANGE, SLICED INTO THIN SEGMENTS

❷ EQUIPMENT

DIGITAL SCALES

MEASURING JUG

6 MINI LOAF CASES

6 PLASTIC SPOONS

❸ METHOD

In a jug, mix the gin, tonic water and orange blossom water. Divide the mixture between the mini loaf cases. Freeze for 30 minutes, add the edible flowers and orange slices, then freeze for 12–14 hours, until solid.

SERVES 6
The classic G&T is elevated with the addition of flowers and orange blossom.

POM, BLACKBERRY & ROSEMARY

❶ INGREDIENTS

200 ML (7 FL OZ) POMEGRANATE JUICE
½ POMEGRANATE (SEEDS ONLY)
60 ML (2 FL OZ) VODKA
400 ML (13½ FL OZ) SODA WATER
50 ML (1¾ FL OZ) LIGHT AGAVE SYRUP
200 G (7 OZ) BLACKBERRIES, HALVED
12 SHORT ROSEMARY STALKS

❷ EQUIPMENT

DIGITAL SCALES   MEASURING JUG   12 MINI POPSICLE MOULDS & STICKS

❸ METHOD

In a jug, mix the pomegranate juice and the seeds and divide between the popsicle moulds. Place the lid on the tray and freeze overnight. Mix the vodka, soda water and agave syrup in a jug. Remove the frozen pops and add 2-3 blackberries to each mould, then pour in the vodka-soda mixture. Insert a rosemary stalk into each mould and freeze for 12–14 hours, until solid.

SERVES 12
These mini pops are very impressive. The infused rosemary really enhances the flavour.

NB: You'll need to start this recipe the day before.

BLUEBERRY LAVENDER POP

SERVES 8
Blueberries have among the highest antioxidant count of any berry. Pairing them with an aromatic, floral herb like lavender gives them a summery flavour.

❶ INGREDIENTS

400 G (14 OZ) FROZEN BLUEBERRIES
1 TABLESPOON BLUEBERRY POWDER (OPTIONAL)
150 ML (5 FL OZ) CLUB SODA • 100 ML (3½ FL OZ) VODKA
20 ML (¾ FL OZ) ELDERFLOWER LIQUEUR
2 TEASPOONS DRIED EDIBLE LAVENDER FLOWERS

❷ EQUIPMENT

BLENDER   DIGITAL SCALES   MEASURING JUG   8 POPSICLE MOULDS & STICKS

❸ METHOD

Blitz the blueberries and blueberry powder (if using) in a blender or food processor until smooth. Pour into a jug, add the club soda, vodka and elderflower liqueur, and stir. Add the lavender flowers to each popsicle mould, divide the mixture between them, place the lid on the tray, and freeze for 30 minutes. Then slide the popsicle sticks into the lid slots and freeze for a further 12–14 hours, until solid.

JASMINE & LEMONGRASS POP

❶ INGREDIENTS

3 LEMONGRASS STALKS, BRUISED,
WITH SOME SHARDS RESERVED
60 ML (2 FL OZ) LIGHT AGAVE SYRUP
100 ML (3½ FL OZ) VODKA • 4 JASMINE TEA BAGS
550 ML (18½ FL OZ) JUST-BOILED WATER

❷ EQUIPMENT

DIGITAL
SCALES

MEASURING
JUG

8 POPSICLE
MOULDS & STICKS

❸ METHOD

Place the bruised lemongrass, agave syrup,
vodka and the jasmine tea bags in a jug.
Pour in the just-boiled water, stir and allow
to cool. Once completely cooled, discard the
tea bags and lemongrass. Divide the mixture
between the popsicle moulds, place the lid
on the tray, and freeze for 30 minutes. Then
slide the reserved lemongrass shards into the
lid slots and freeze for a further 12–14 hours,
until solid. Flip the moulds over and run under
warm water to release the popsicles.

SERVES 8
Jasmine tea and fresh lemongrass pair
beautifully in this light and delicate
iced pop.

THAI COCO-POP

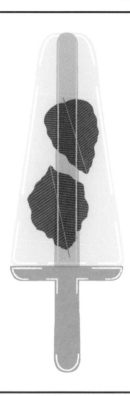

SERVES 8

This Thai-inspired coconut pop is all about the fresh kaffir lime leaves. The best place to source them is in any good Asian grocery store.

❶ INGREDIENTS

100 ML (3½ FL OZ) MALIBU RUM
550 ML (18½ FL OZ) COCONUT WATER
8 KAFFIR LIME LEAVES (FRESH OR DRIED)
JUICE OF 1 LIME

❷ EQUIPMENT

DIGITAL SCALES · MEASURING JUG · 8 POPSICLE MOULDS & STICKS

❸ METHOD

In a jug, mix the Malibu and coconut water together. Divide the mixture between the popsicle moulds and freeze for 30 minutes. Then place the lid on the tray, and freeze for a further 30 minutes. Add a lime leaf to each mould, then slide the sticks into the lid slots and freeze for a further 12–14 hours, until solid.

ARISTOCRAT

Not just for the blue bloods... this pop will have you feeling noble.

SERVES 8

❶ INGREDIENTS

50 ml (1¾ fl oz) dry gin

200 ml (7 fl oz) sparkling wine

300 ml (10 fl oz) soda water

100 g (3½ oz) runny honey

8 lovage leaves

❷ EQUIPMENT

measuring jug
digital scales
8 popsicle moulds
8 popsicle sticks

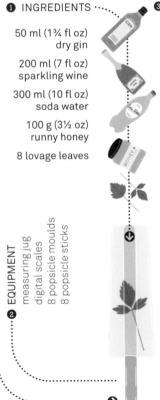

❸ METHOD

In a jug, mix the gin, sparkling wine, soda water and runny honey well. Place 1 lovage leaf in each popsicle mould. Divide the mixture between the popsicle moulds, place the lid on the tray, and freeze for 30 minutes. Slide the popsicle sticks into the lid slots and freeze for a further 12–14 hours, until solid.

MAPLE LEAF

Perfect for the autumn. The lovage adds an interesting light, celery-like flavour.

SERVES 8

❶ INGREDIENTS

100 ml (3½ fl oz) bourbon

2 teaspoons vanilla paste

100 ml (3½ fl oz) maple syrup

300 ml (10 fl oz) cloudy lemonade

2 dashes of Angostura bitters

8 lovage leaves (optional)

❷ EQUIPMENT

measuring jug
digital scales
8 popsicle moulds
8 popsicle sticks

❸ METHOD

In a jug, mix the bourbon, vanilla paste and maple syrup, making sure the syrup dissolves. Next add the lemonade and bitters and mix well. Divide the mixture between the popsicle moulds, place the lid on the tray, and freeze for 30 minutes. Add a lovage leaf to each mould (if desired), slide the popsicle sticks into the lid slots and freeze for a further 12–14 hours, until solid.

THE ROSE GARDEN

This lightly floral ice pop, with lychee, Japanese yuzu and rose, is ultra refreshing.

SERVES 8

❶ INGREDIENTS

100 ml (3½ fl oz) gin

30 ml (1 fl oz) rose water

500 ml (17 fl oz) lychee juice

few dashes of bitters

few dashes of yuzu juice (optional)

edible dried rose petals, to serve

❷ EQUIPMENT
measuring jug
digital scales
8 popsicle moulds
8 popsicle sticks

❸ METHOD
In a jug, mix the gin, rose water, lychee juice, bitters and yuzu juice. Divide the mixture between the popsicle moulds, place the lid on the tray, and freeze for 30 minutes. Add a pinch of dried rose petals to each mould, slide the popsicle sticks into the lid slots and freeze for a further 12–14 hours, until solid. Sprinkle with extra rose petals before serving.

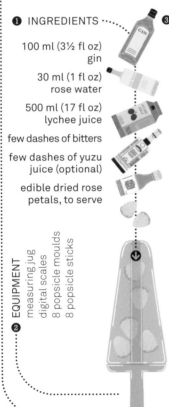

BLOODY ROSEMARY

Rosemary, with its slight woodiness, and blood orange, with its intense and sweet citrus, are perfect partners in this pop.

SERVES 8

❶ INGREDIENTS

500 ml (17 fl oz) blood orange juice

100 ml (3½ fl oz) vodka

80 g (2¾ oz) runny honey

8 rosemary stalks

1 blood orange, thinly sliced

❷ EQUIPMENT
measuring jug
digital scales
8 popsicle moulds
8 popsicle sticks

❸ METHOD
In a jug, mix together the blood orange juice, vodka and honey. Divide the mixture between the popsicle moulds, place the lid on the tray, and freeze for 30 minutes. Then slide the rosemary stalks, blood orange slices and popsicle sticks into the lid slots and freeze for a further 12–14 hours, until solid. Flip the moulds over and run under warm water to release the popsicles.

FENNEL GIN

SERVES 8
This aromatic fennel gin poptail is a different take on the traditional gin and tonic.

❶ INGREDIENTS

1 FENNEL BULB, SLICED LENGTHWAYS INTO LONG WEDGES, RESERVING THE FRONDS
60 ML (2 FL OZ) GIN
40 ML (1¼ FL OZ) CHARTREUSE
60 ML (2 FL OZ) LIGHT AGAVE SYRUP
JUICE OF 1 LEMON
500 ML (17 FL OZ) CLUB SODA

❷ EQUIPMENT

DIGITAL SCALES   MEASURING JUG   8 POPSICLE MOULDS & STICKS

❸ METHOD

Start by inserting the fennel with the fronds into the popsicle moulds, then set aside. Meanwhile, in a jug, mix the gin, Chartreuse, agave syrup, lemon juice and club soda. Divide the mixture between the moulds, place the lid on the tray, and freeze for 30 minutes. Then slide the popsicle sticks into the lid slots and freeze for a further 12–14 hours, until solid.

FLORABOTANICA

This punchy pop is finished with dried flowers.

SERVES 8

Ingredients
70 ml (2¼ fl oz) gin
30 ml (1 fl oz) Midori
50 ml (1¾ fl oz) yuzu juice
10 ml (¼ fl oz) rose water
dash of bitters
1 teaspoon Maraschino cherry syrup
450 ml (15 fl oz) club soda
edible dried flower petals, such cornflower or rose

Equipment
measuring jug, digital scales,
8 popsicle moulds, 8 popsicle sticks

Method
In a jug, mix the gin, Midori, yuzu juice, rose water,
bitters and Maraschino syrup with the club soda.
Add a pinch of dried flowers to each popsicle
mould. Divide the mixture between the moulds,
and freeze for 30 minutes. Then insert the sticks
and freeze for a further 12–14 hours, until solid.

GIRL ATTACK

This is a classic girls' night in cocktail, but turned
into a poptail it's even better!

SERVES 8

Ingredients
100 ml (3½ fl oz) Frangelico
juice of 3 limes, plus 1 lime sliced into rounds
dash of orange blossom water
500 ml (17 fl oz) sugar-free lemonade
8 kaffir lime leaves

Equipment
measuring jug, digital scales,
8 popsicle moulds, 8 popsicle sticks

Method
In a jug, mix the Frangelico, lime juice, orange
blossom water and lemonade. Divide the mixture
between the popsicle moulds, place the lid on the
tray, and freeze for 30 minutes. Then add the
lime slices and kaffir leaves, slide the popsicle
sticks into the lid slots and freeze for a further
12–14 hours, until solid.

KATHY KORDALIS

Kathy Kordalis is a London-based food-stylist and recipe writer. She has worked in the food industry for years and her experience includes managing the Divertimenti Cookery School and training as a chef at the Leiths School of Food and Wine. Her approach to food is light, relaxed and accessible, drawing inspiration from her classical training in London, along with her Australian and Mediterranean heritage. It's all about sharing with friends and family, and coming up with new recipes to excite them!

ACKNOWLEDGEMENTS

Thank you to Kate Pollard, Kajal Mistry and the wonderful team at Hardie Grant. Stuart Hardie for the design and Esme Lonsdale for the illustrations. And thank you to Matthew for tasting every single one of the 90 poptails, and to my family the world over.

INDEX

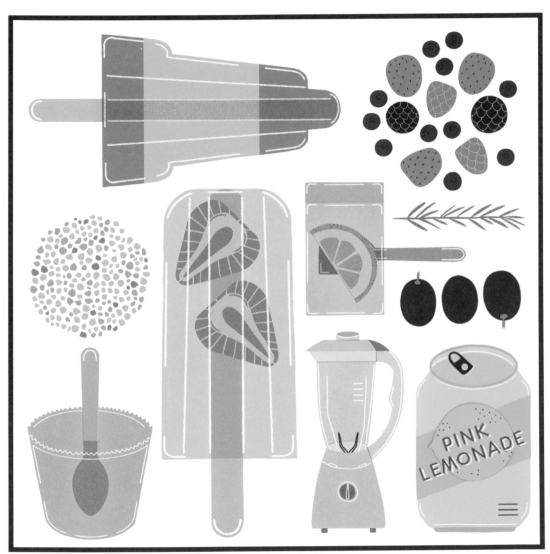

The Poptail Manual by Kathy Kordalis

First published in 2017 by Hardie Grant Books

Hardie Grant Books (UK)
5th Floor
52–54 Southwark Street
London, SE1 1UN
hardiegrant.co.uk

Hardie Grant Books (Australia)
Ground Floor, Building 1
658 Church Street
Melbourne, VIC 3121
hardiegrant.com.au

British Library Cataloguing-in-Publication Data.
A catalogue record for this book is available from the British Library.

ISBN 978-1-78488-093-4

Publisher: Kate Pollard
Commissioning Editor: Kajal Mistry
Editorial Assistant: Hannah Roberts
Publishing Assistant: Eila Purvis
Cover and Internal Design: Stuart Hardie
Illustrator: Esme Lonsdale
Copy Editor: Kate Wanwimolruk
Indexer: Cathy Heath
Colour Reproduction by p2d

Printed and bound in China by 1010

10 9 8 7 6 5 4 3 2 1